Let's Cook

Shirley Sydenham

illustrated by Carol Pelham-Thorman

Contents

Healthy eating	3
French toast	4
Bacon-and-egg in a bun	5
An Italian festa!	6
Spaghetti with mushroom sauce	6
Easy pizza	8
Have a barbeque	9
Malaysian satay	9
Salad	10
Corn on the cob	11
Honey-baked bananas	12
Fruit cup	13
Family dinner for four	14
Menu	14
Working order	15
Bean and bacon soup	16
Orange-honey chicken	17
Baked jacket potatoes	18
Greek-style beans	19
Fun food	20
Funny faces	20
Pear mice in jelly	21
Ca-bana the dragon	22
Mr G. Raffe	23
Using pastry sheets	24
Cheeseless cheesecakes	24
Mini quiches	25
Super scone ideas	26
Plain scones	26
Sultana scones	27
Cheesy scone roll	28
Fruity roll	29
Carrot cake	30
German cake	31
An international biscuit feast	32
Kourabiedes: Greek shortbreads	32
Russian sugar cookies	33
Chinese and Vietnamese almond biscuits	34
American chocolate cookies	36
Ice cream	37
We all scream for ice cream!	37
Baked Alaska	38
Clown sundaes for any day	39
Top-of-the-pyramid sweet treats	40
Chocolate roughs	40
Coconut ice	41
Apricot balls	42
Gift-giving ideas	43
Glossary of equipment	44
Glossary of ingredients	46
Glossary of cooking words	48

Healthy eating

DAILY FOOD PYRAMID

A healthy kid's daily food should form a pyramid shape.

You eat just a little from this section each day.

You eat a moderate amount from this section.

Most of what you eat each day comes from this section.

The food pyramid is the basis of a healthy *balanced* diet.

This is an *unbalanced* daily diet.

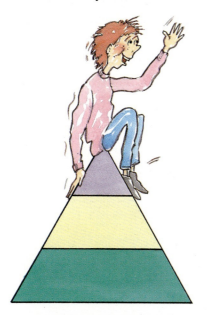

French toast

Ingredients:
1 egg
½ cup milk
2 slices bread
a little butter or margarine
syrup, sugar or honey

Things you need:
bowl
fork
frying pan
spatula
plate

1. Beat the egg and milk together in the bowl.
2. Put a slice of bread into the bowl and make sure it gets well soaked.
3. Heat the frying pan over a medium heat and put a small lump of butter in.
4. When the butter is sizzling and completely melted, take the bread from the bowl and place it in the pan.
5. While this slice is cooking, put the second slice into the bowl to soak.
6. After about 1 minute, or when the cooked side is brown, turn the slice over and let it brown on the other side.
7. When both sides are done, put the toast on the plate, sizzle some more butter in the pan and start cooking the second piece.
8. Sprinkle your French toast with sugar, or pour some honey or syrup over it.

Bacon-and-egg in a bun

Ingredients:
4 round bread rolls
butter or margarine
salt and pepper
dried thyme
4 eggs
2 rashers bacon (chopped)
grated cheddar cheese

Things you need:
knife
tongs

1. Cut a round hole in the top of each bread roll, a bit larger than a 50c coin.
2. With your fingers, remove some of the bread from inside to make the hole larger.
3. Butter the insides of the buns and sprinkle in a little salt, pepper and thyme.
4. Crack an egg into each bun.
5. Pop the buns under the griller, set fairly low so that bread doesn't burn while the eggs are cooking.
6. When the eggs are cooked (the white will not be clear and runny any more), fill the tops of the holes with the chopped bacon, then grated cheese. Put them under the griller set on a medium heat.
7. When the bacon and cheese are bubbling, the buns are done. You'll need to use a knife and fork to eat these.

An Italian festa!

Spaghetti with mushroom sauce

Ingredients:
4 tablespoons vegetable oil
4 tablespoons butter
2 onions
500 g mushrooms
1 clove garlic
salt and pepper
500 g tomatoes
½ teaspoon dried oregano
500 g spaghetti (thick or thin, flat or round, plain or coloured!)
extra butter
grated parmesan cheese

Things you need:
2 large saucepans
fork
knife
serving bowl
colander

1. Chop the onions, garlic and the tomatoes. Slice the mushrooms.
2. Heat the oil and butter in a saucepan, add the onions and garlic and fry them gently until they're soft.

3. Add the mushrooms, salt and pepper, and cook them over a medium heat for 10 minutes.
4. Add the tomatoes and oregano, and simmer for 30 minutes.
5. Half-fill the other saucepan with water, add ½ teaspoon salt, and bring it to a boil over high heat.
6. When the water is bubbling, put in the spaghetti, broken in half if you like. It sinks down as it softens in the water.
7. Put the lid half on and turn down the heat so that it keeps bubbling but doesn't boil over. After 15–20 minutes, take out a strand with a fork and taste it to see if it is cooked through.
8. Empty the spaghetti into a colander and drain it.
9. Put the spaghetti into a big bowl and add some butter, stirring it through.
10. Pour the mushroom sauce over the spaghetti and have the parmesan cheese ready for people to sprinkle over their helpings.

Easy pizza

Ingredients:
2 tomatoes
1 onion
2 cloves garlic
1 or 2 tablespoons tomato paste
vegetable oil
2 Lebanese flatbreads
slices of mozzarella cheese
your choice of toppings: cabana, salami, anchovies, capsicums, shrimps, clams, mushrooms, black olives.

Things you need:
saucepan
knife
baking tray
wooden spoon

1. Slice the onion, garlic and tomatoes.
2. Heat 1 tablespoon of oil in a saucepan, and fry the onions and garlic until they're soft.
3. Add the tomatoes and tomato paste, oregano and about ½ cup water, and simmer gently for about 10 minutes. This sauce can be made well ahead.
4. Turn the oven on to 200°C.
5. Put the 2 flatbreads on the baking tray and spread the tomato mixture over them both.
6. Arrange your choice of toppings all over the tomato mixture.
7. Cover the pizzas with slices of mozzarella cheese.
8. Trickle about 1 tablespoon of oil all over the pizzas and pop the baking tray into the oven.
9. After 10–15 minutes, the cheese should be bubbly with brown patches, and is ready to be cut into wedges and eaten!

Have a barbeque

Malaysian satay

Ingredients:
1 kg beef, pork or chicken
1½ teaspoons Chinese five-spice powder
½ teaspoon ground ginger
1½ teaspoons ground cumin
½ teaspoon ground coriander
3 cloves garlic
2 small onions
2 teaspoons light soy
4 teaspoons sugar
2 teaspoons oil
½ teaspoon salt

Things you need:
16–18 bamboo skewers, soaked for several hours so they don't burn
bowl
knife
tongs

1. Cut the meat or chicken into small cubes, about 1 cm square, and put them in the bowl.
2. Cut the onions and garlic into small pieces and add them to the bowl.
3. Put in all the other ingredients, mix everything together well and leave the bowl for about an hour.
4. Fill the skewers with the meat or chicken and cook them on a hot barbeque for several minutes, turning them over several times.

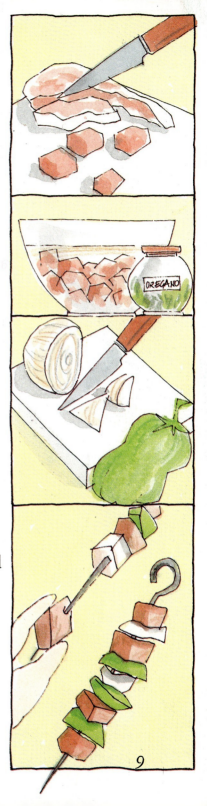

Salad

Ingredients:
1 small lettuce (or ½ big one!)
½ cucumber
2 tomatoes, or a lot of cherry tomatoes
a handful of alfalfa sprouts
1 small green capsicum
any other vegies you like: celery, broccoli, mushrooms, olives, carrots, whatever! Go wild!
bought salad dressing (French or Italian)

Things you need:
large salad bowl
salad servers
knife

1. Wash all the vegetables.
2. Tear the lettuce into pieces and put them in the bowl.
3. Slice all the other ingredients, except the sprouts and cherry tomatoes if you use them, and add them all to the bowl.
4. Just before serving, pour over about ¼ cup dressing and carefully toss the salad around in the bowl with the servers so that everything gets lightly coated.

Corn on the cob

Ingredients:
4 corn cobs, still with the husks
 (the leaf-like covering)
Butter or margarine

Things you need:
string and scissors
tongs

1. Peel back the green husks and remove all the silky strands from underneath.
2. Pull the husks back into place and tie a piece of string around the top to keep them in place.
3. Soak the corn in cold water for 1 hour before cooking.
4. Put the corn cobs onto the barbeque and cook them for 15 minutes, turning them several times.
5. Remove the burnt husks and throw them away.
6. Dot the corn with dobs of butter or margarine.

Honey-baked bananas

Ingredients:
4 ripe bananas
4 heaped teaspoons brown sugar
4 teaspoons honey
juice of 1 lemon
grated lemon rind

Things you need:
4 squares of foil large
 enough to wrap a
 banana in
tongs
grater
teaspoon

1. Place a peeled banana on each square of foil.
2. Squeeze lemon juice over each banana.
3. Sprinkle each with grated lemon rind and brown sugar.
4. Dribble a teaspoon of honey over each.
5. Wrap each banana in its foil.
6. Place the foil parcels on the barbeque for 5–10 minutes.

Fruit cup

Ingredients:
¼ litre cold tea
½ cup caster sugar
¼ cup hot water
2 lemons
500 ml pine-orange juice
500 ml grapefruit juice
1 bottle dry ginger ale
½ bottle lemonade
pieces of fruit to float about

Things you need:
large bowl
ladle
juice squeezer
spoon

1. Dissolve the sugar in the water.
2. Squeeze the lemons.
3. Mix everything together in the bowl.
4. Add the fruit and some ice cubes, and it's ready!

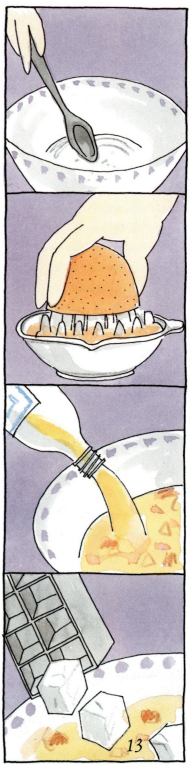

Family dinner for four

Are you ready to try cooking dinner for the family? The recipes are for four, so you may have to increase or decrease quantities. This is for the weekend or for holidays.

Working order

Well ahead of time (morning, early afternoon, or even the day before):
1. Choose an ice cream recipe from page 37, prepare it according to the recipe and put it in the freezer.
2. Using the recipe on page 16, make the soup so that all you have to do is reheat it.

About 2 hours before dinner:
1. Wash all the fresh vegetables and dry them with paper towel.
2. Steps 2–4, page 19.
3. Step 5, page 18.

About 1 hour before dinner:
1. Prepare the oven. Make sure you have one shelf in the middle of the oven and one just below it. Turn the oven on to 180°C.
2. Steps 2–6, page 17.
3. Steps 2–3, page 18.

About 15 minutes after putting the chicken in the oven:
1. Put the soup on a low flame to heat.
2. Step 7, page 17.
3. Steps 5–8, page 19.

About 30 minutes after putting the chicken in the oven:
1. Steps 8–10, page 17.
2. Step 4, page 18.
3. Serve the soup and sit down and enjoy it.
4. After the soup serve the main course.
5. After that, serve the ice cream.
6. After that . . . relax! Well done!

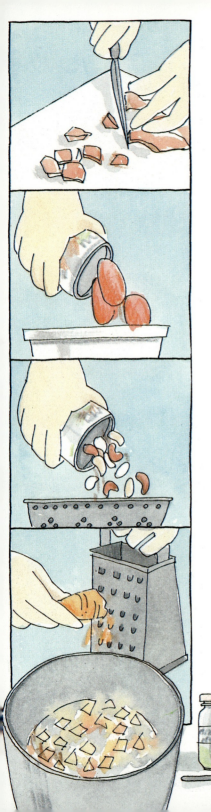

Bean and bacon soup

Ingredients:
1 tablespoon oil
250 g bacon pieces
2 onions
1 tin tomatoes (400 g)
1 tin three bean mix (440 g)
1 litre water
2 chicken stock cubes
½ teaspoon dried basil
½ teaspoon mixed herbs
2 cloves garlic
2 carrots

Things you need:
knife
bowl
fork
colander
grater
vegetable peeler
large saucepan
measuring jug

1. Cut the bacon pieces smaller if they are too big, and chop up the onions and garlic.
2. Empty the tin of tomatoes into a bowl and mash them up with a fork.
3. Empty the tin of beans into a colander and let the liquid drain away.
4. Peel and grate the carrots.
5. Heat the oil in the saucepan and fry the bacon for a few minutes.
6. Add the onions and garlic and cook until the onions are soft.
7. Add the basil and mixed herbs, and all the other ingredients.
8. Cover the pan and simmer the soup for 15 minutes.

Orange–honey chicken

Ingredients:
4 chicken pieces
60 g butter
2 tablespoons honey
¼ cup orange juice
2 teaspoons grated orange rind

Things you need:
baking dish
juice squeezer
grater, knife
small saucepan
oven mitts
tongs, large spoon

1. Preheat the oven to 180°C.
2. Place the chicken pieces in the baking dish with the skin side down.
3. Cut the butter into little pieces and sprinkle the pieces all over the chicken.
4. Put the baking dish into the oven and leave it for 30 minutes.
5. Meanwhile, squeeze the orange juice and grate the rind.
6. Put the juice, rind and honey into the small saucepan.
7. Heat the orange–honey mixture gently until it begins to bubble, then turn off the heat.
8. After the chicken has been in for 30 minutes, carefully take the dish from the oven, and turn the pieces over with the tongs.
9. Pour the orange–honey mixture over the chicken.
10. Return the chicken to the oven for about 20 minutes more. When you serve the chicken, put 1 piece on each plate and spoon over some of the orange–honey mixture.

Baked jacket potatoes

Ingredients:
4 medium potatoes
vegetable oil
sour cream or plain yoghurt
a bunch of chives or 3 shallots

Things you need:
paper towel
tongs

1. Wash the potatoes and pat them dry with a paper towel.
2. Dampen some more paper towel with the oil and wipe each potato to coat it lightly with oil.
3. Place the potatoes in a row along the front of an oven shelf so that they are not touching each other.
4. After about 20 minutes, turn them over with tongs and leave them in for another 20 minutes or so.
5. Mix the chopped chives or shallots with the sour cream or yoghurt. Pop the mixture into the refrigerator and when you're ready to serve dinner put it in a little bowl on the table so people can dob some onto their potatoes.

Greek-style beans

Ingredients:
350 g green beans
2 medium onions
2 cloves garlic
salt and pepper
2 tablespoons oil
2 tomatoes

Things you need:
colander
knife
medium-sized saucepan
3 small bowls or saucers

1. Wash the beans in the colander and wash the tomatoes.
2. Break off the ends of the beans and break them in half.
3. Slice the onions, chop the garlic and cut the tomatoes into small chunks.
4. Keep the chopped garlic, onions, beans and tomatoes in separate bowls until you're ready to cook them.
5. Heat the oil in the saucepan and cook the onions over a low heat until they are soft.
6. Add the beans and mix them in with the onions.
7. Add the tomatoes, garlic and a sprinkle of salt and pepper.
8. Cover the saucepan and simmer for 15 minutes.

Fun food

Funny faces

Ingredients:
large round crackers
cheddar cheese spread or a pinkish meat paste
Bits and pieces for hair and faces: alfalfa sprouts, parsley, sliced stuffed olives, capsicum, carrot slices, gherkin or other pickles, tomato . . . use your imagination!

Things you need:
knife

1. Spread the crackers with cheese spread or meat paste, and press on all sorts of foods to make faces.

Here are some suggestions for starters:

parsley
olive slices
carrot slice
tomato

gherkin slivers
cheese "single"
carrot sliver
½ carrot slice

grated carrot
gherkin slices
tip of cheese stick
red capsicum

alfalfa sprouts
sultanas
gherkin tip
tomato

Pear mice in jelly

Ingredients:
1 large tin pear halves
1 packet green jelly
1 flat licorice strap, from which you cut a tail and two ears for each pear half
whole cloves, 3 per pear half

Things you need:
tin opener
colander
bowl
spoon
measuring jug
large serving dish (flat)

1. Empty the jelly crystals into a bowl and pour 1 cup of boiling water over them.
2. Stir until the crystals have completely dissolved, then add 1 cup of cold water.
3. Put the jelly into the refrigerator to set.
4. When the jelly is set, prepare the mice. Open the tin and gently drain the pears. Put two clove eyes and a clove nose into the small end of each pear, and two licorice ears. Cut tails from licorice and put them into slits at the big end of the pears.
5. Break up the jelly and spread the chunks around the serving dish, then arrange the mice on the dish amongst the clumps of jelly.

Ca-bana the Dragon

Ingredients:
1 piece of cabana (about 12 cm long)
1 cheese "single"
1 cheese wedge or triangle
4 stuffed olives
the pointy tip of a carrot (about 2 cm long)
1 stick celery (about 6 cm long and cut from the top end)
4 cloves
4 slices of apple and a piece of red apple peel, cut in a spiral

Things you need:
toothpicks for joining the pieces together
knife
vegetable peeler

1. Cut a groove along the cabana, so that triangles cut from the cheese "single" will stand up along the dragon's back.
2. Cut a wedge of cheese for the head.
3. Cut the apple slices into clawed foot shapes.
4. Cut 4 triangles from the cheese "single" . . . three for the back and one for the end of the tail.
5. Using toothpicks to join the pieces, assemble the dragon like the picture below:

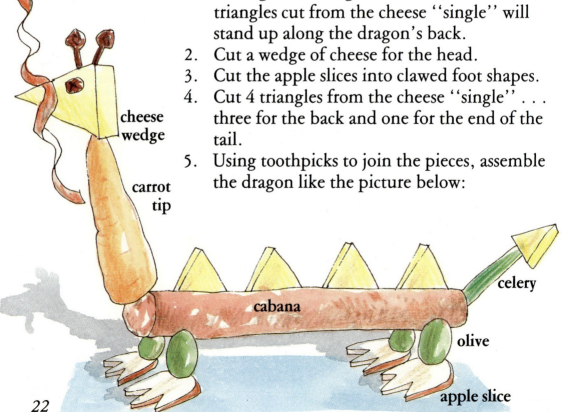

Mr G. Raffe

Ingredients:
1 piece cabana (about 8 cm long)
1 cheese stick
4 celery sticks (about 10 cm long)
2 little celery stalks with leafy bits
small parsley sprig
1 cheese triangle or wedge
2 slices of stuffed olive

Things you need:
toothpicks for joining the pieces together
knife

Using the toothpicks to join the pieces together, assemble the giraffe as the picture shows:

Using pastry sheets

CHEESELESS CHEESECAKES!

Ingredients:
90 g sugar
90 g soft butter
90 g mixed peel
3 egg yolks (use the whites for baked Alaska!)
apricot jam
ready-rolled shortcrust pastry sheets

Things you need:
cupcake baking tin
round biscuit cutter a little larger than the cupcake shapes
bowl
wooden spoon
teaspoon
rack
egg separator

1. Preheat the oven to 230°C.
2. Grease the cupcake tin, cut pastry circles and line each cupcake shape with pastry.
3. Put the butter and sugar in a bowl and stir them until creamy.
4. Stir in the egg yolks and mixed peel.
5. Put about ½ teaspoon of apricot jam into each cupcake.
6. Put 1 teaspoonful of filling on top of the jam in each cupcake.
7. Turn the oven down to 150°C, and bake the cheese- cakes for about 20 minutes or until they are golden.
8. Put the cheesecakes on a rack to cool.

Mini quiches (pronounced "keeshes")

Ingredients:
Ready-rolled shortcrust pastry
   sheets
125 g grated cheese
125 g ham
3 tablespoons cream
1 tablespoon French mustard
1 egg
salt and pepper

Things you need:
cupcake baking tray
round biscuit cutter a
   little larger than
   the cupcake
   shapes
grater
bowl
knife
teaspoon

1. Turn the oven on to 200°C and grease the cupcake tin.
2. Cut pastry circles and line the cupcake shapes with pastry.
3. Chop the ham into tiny pieces and put them in a bowl.
4. Grate the cheese and add it to the ham.
5. Mix in the cream, mustard, egg, salt and pepper.
6. Put about 2 teaspoonfuls of the mixture into each pastry cupcake.
7. Bake for 20 minutes, or until the filling is puffed up and browned.
8. These are served hot, straight from the oven.

Super scone ideas

Plain scones

Ingredients:
2 cups self-raising flour
½ teaspoon salt
2 tablespoons butter or margarine
½ cup milk
¼ cup water
1 tablespoon milk, extra

Things you need:
sifter
large bowl
scone cutter
baking tray
pastry brush
knife
oven mitts
rack and spatula

1. Turn oven on to 230°C and grease baking tray.
2. Sift flour and salt into a bowl.
3. Put in the butter or margarine and rub it into the flour with your fingers until the mixture looks like breadcrumbs.
4. Mix the milk and water together and pour it into the flour, mixing it into a soft dough with the knife.
5. Tip the dough onto a floury surface and press and roll it until it is smooth on the outside.

6. Pat the dough out to about 2 cm thick.
7. Dip the scone cutter into flour and then press it into the dough. Cut out as many as you can, then pat the dough out again and keep cutting.
8. Put all the scones onto the baking tray, close together but not touching.
9. Brush the tops with the extra milk, and bake them for 10–15 minutes until they are golden brown.
10. Take the tray out of the oven and lift the scones onto a wire rack to cool.
11. Serve them warm with butter and jam, or cold with jam and whipped cream.

Sultana scones

The recipe is the same as the plain scones, but after you have rubbed the butter or margarine into the flour, add:

   3 tablespoons sugar and
   ½ cup sultanas.

Then continue as with the plain scones.

Cheesy scone roll

Ingredients:
1 batch of plain scone dough — recipe on page 26
125 g grated cheddar cheese
50 g grated parmesan cheese
2 teaspoons mustard
8 shallots
2 tablespoons butter or margarine
1 tablespoon butter or margarine, extra

Things you need:
bowl
pastry brush
small saucepan
baking tray
spoon
knife
chopping block

1. Turn the oven on to 230°C and grease the baking tray.
2. Chop the shallots and mix them with the grated cheeses and the mustard.
3. Mix in the butter until the mixture comes together in a ball.
4. Pat the scone dough out to a rectangle of about 1 cm thick.
5. Melt the extra butter and brush it all over the dough.
6. Spread the filling evenly over the dough.
7. Starting at one of the long sides, carefully roll up the dough just like a jam roll cake.
8. Put the roll onto the greased baking tray, either straight or curved into a circle, and brush the top with milk.
9. Bake in the oven for 10–15 minutes or until it is golden brown.

Fruity roll

Ingredients:
1 batch plain scone dough — recipe on page 26
60 g butter or margarine (soft)
⅓ cup brown sugar
½ cup sultanas
½ cup currants
60 g glacé cherries
60 g mixed peel
1 teaspoon cinnamon
milk

Things you need:
bowl
rolling pin
pastry brush
baking tray
wooden spoon
knife

1. Turn the oven on to 180°C and grease the baking tray.
2. On a floury surface, roll out the dough to a rectangle about 1 cm thick.
3. In a bowl, stir the butter and sugar together until they're creamy.
4. Spread the butter and sugar mixture over the dough.
5. Sprinkle the fruit evenly all over, then the cinnamon.
6. Starting at one of the long ends, roll up the dough.
7. Slice the roll into about 10 or 12 slices, and put them onto the baking tray, close but not touching.
8. Brush the rounds with milk and bake them for 25–30 minutes, or until they're golden brown.

Carrot cake

Ingredients:
2 cups sugar (preferably raw)
2 cups self-raising flour
1 cup vegetable oil
4 eggs
3 teaspoons cinnamon
1 teaspoon salt
½ cup walnut pieces
3 cups grated raw carrot

Things you need:
grater
large mixing bowl
wooden spoon
large round cake tin
fork
oven mitts
rack
skewer

1. Turn the oven on to 150°C and grease the cake tin.
2. Beat the eggs with a fork, and mix in the sugar and oil.
3. Sift the flour, salt and cinnamon into the mixture, and stir well.
4. Stir in the nuts and grated carrot.
5. Pour the mixture into the cake tin and bake it for 50–60 minutes. You'll know it's done when it starts coming away from the side of the tin. And when you poke a skewer into the centre it should come out with nothing stuck to it.
6. Turn the cagke out onto a wire rack to cool.

German cake

Ingredients:
125 g butter (soft)
175 g caster sugar
1 egg
250 g plain flour
¼ teaspoon baking powder
pinch of salt
30 g blanched almonds
jam (raspberry or blackberry)

Things you need:
cake tin (18 cm sandwich tin)
bowl
sifter
wooden spoon
knife
rack

1. Preheat the oven to 180°C and grease the cake tin.
2. Stir the butter until it is creamy, then stir in the sugar.
3. Add the egg and mix well.
4. Gradually add the sifted flour, baking powder and salt, mixing it to quite a stiff dough.
5. Press half the mixture into the cake tin.
6. Spread it with jam.
7. Press the rest of the mixture on top and press the almonds in a pattern around the cake.
8. Bake for ¾–1 hour.
9. Take it out of the oven and leave it for about 5 minutes before tipping it out onto a rack.

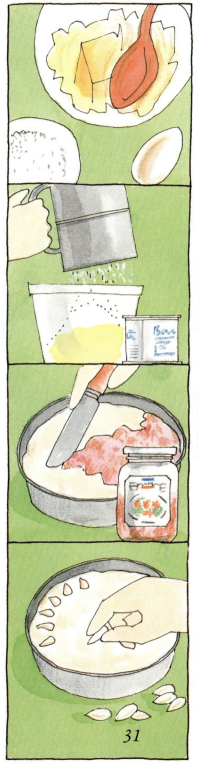

An international biscuit feast

Kourabiedes: Greek shortbreads

Ingredients:
2 cups plain flour
1 cup rice flour
1 cup icing sugar
250 g butter
extra icing sugar

Things you need:
bowl
sifter
plastic wrap
rolling pin
oven mitts
baking tray
rack, spatula
knife

1. Grease the baking tray and turn the oven on to 150°C.
2. Sift flour, ground rice and icing sugar into the bowl.
3. Add the butter in chunks and mix it with your fingers until it forms a stiff dough.
4. Wrap the dough in plastic wrap and chill it in the refrigerator for about 10 minutes.
5. Roll out the dough on a floury surface to form a rectangle about ½ cm thick.
6. Cut the dough into strips about 8 cm long and 2 cm wide and arrange them on the baking tray.
7. Bake them in the oven for about 45 minutes, without letting them brown.
8. Take the tray out of the oven and leave the biscuits on the tray for 2 minutes before carefully lifting them onto the rack.
9. While they are still warm, dip the biscuits into the extra icing sugar.

Russian sugar cookies

Ingredients:
125 g sugar
250 g butter (soft)
¼ teaspoon salt
3 eggs
3 tablespoons sour cream
½ teaspoon grated lemon rind
1 teaspoon lemon juice
400 g plain flour
¼ teaspoon bicarbonate of soda
extra sugar

Things you need:
bowl
wooden spoon
rolling pin
baking tray
rack
spatula
oven mitts
knife
juice squeezer
grater

1. Turn the oven on to 230°C and grease the baking tray.
2. In the bowl, stir the butter to make it creamy, then stir in the sugar and salt.
3. Add the beaten eggs, a bit at a time, and stir well.
4. Mix in the sour cream, lemon juice and rind.
5. Slowly mix in the flour and soda.
6. On a floury surface, roll out the dough to about ½ cm thickness, then sprinkle the dough with sugar.
7. Cut the dough into diamonds.
8. Put them onto the baking tray and bake them in the oven for about 8 minutes, or until they are barely gold. Don't let them get brown.
9. Lift them onto the rack to cool.

Chinese and Vietnamese almond biscuits

Ingredients:
100 g blanched almonds
1 teaspoon almond essence
2 teaspoons baking powder
½ teaspoon bicarbonate of soda
1 tablespoon of water
75 g melted butter
1 egg
½ teaspoon salt
100 g brown sugar
200 g plain flour
1 extra egg, beaten

Things you need:
cup
bowl
baking tray
pastry brush
rack
spatula
oven mitts
spoon
small saucepan
plastic wrap
knife

1. In a cup, dissolve the baking powder and bicarbonate of soda in the water.
2. In a bowl, mix together the melted butter, the egg, the salt, the baking powder and soda in water, and the almond essence.
3. Bit by bit, stir in the sugar and the flour, then knead the dough by rolling it into a ball and pressing it down over and over again until the dough is smooth.
4. Divide the dough into three, roll each piece into a cylinder about 4 cm thick.
5. Wrap each cylinder in plastic wrap and put them in the freezer for 30 minutes, or in the refrigerator for 3 hours.
6. Turn the oven on to 180°C and grease the baking tray.
7. Unwrap the rolls of dough and cut them into ½ cm thick slices with a knife dipped in flour.
8. Put the slices on the baking tray, leaving about 2 cm of space around each.
9. Press a blanched almond into the centre of each, and brush the biscuits with the beaten egg.
10. Bake them for about 25 minutes until they are golden, then place them on the rack to cool.

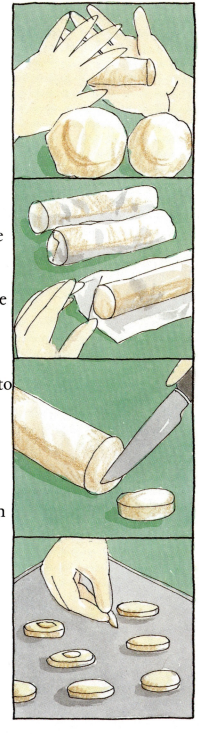

American chocolate cookies

Ingredients:
125 g cooking chocolate
125 g butter
1 egg
175 g brown sugar
175 g self-raising flour

Things you need:
double boiler
bowl
fork
baking tray
rack and spatula
oven mitts

1. Preheat the oven to 200°C and grease the tray.
2. Melt the chocolate; follow the instructions given in the chocolate rough recipe on page 40.
3. Take the chocolate off the heat, add chunks of butter and stir until smooth.
4. Break the egg into the bowl and mix in the sugar, using a fork.
5. Stir the chocolate mixture into the egg mixture.
6. Add the flour slowly and stir until you have a stiff dough.
7. Break off bits of dough and roll them into balls about the size of walnuts.
8. Put the balls, well-spaced, onto the baking tray and bake for 10–12 minutes, or until they have spread out and the tops are covered with cracks.
9. Put them on the rack to cool and crisp.

Ice cream

W<small>E ALL SCREAM FOR ICE CREAM</small>!

For each of these recipes, step 1 is the same: Leave 1 litre of vanilla ice cream out of the freezer for an hour or so until it is soft enough to have delicious extras stirred in. After that, the changed ice cream goes back into the freezer to re-freeze.

CLEVER ICE CREAM
Add a large packet of Smarties to the ice cream . . . but only give a few quick stirs to spread them through the ice cream. Too much stirring makes all the colours mix together, and you won't get lovely trickles of colour through the white ice cream. This looks great served in tall glasses so you can see the rainbows.

FRUIT SALAD ICE CREAM
Chop up lots of favourite fruits to make a super fruit salad, or use tinned fruit salad, or even a combination of both, and stir it through. Don't have the chunks of fruit too large.

ROCKY ROAD ICE CREAM
Chop up marshmallows and red glacé cherries, mix them with lots of chocolate chips and chopped nuts, and stir this mixture into the ice cream.

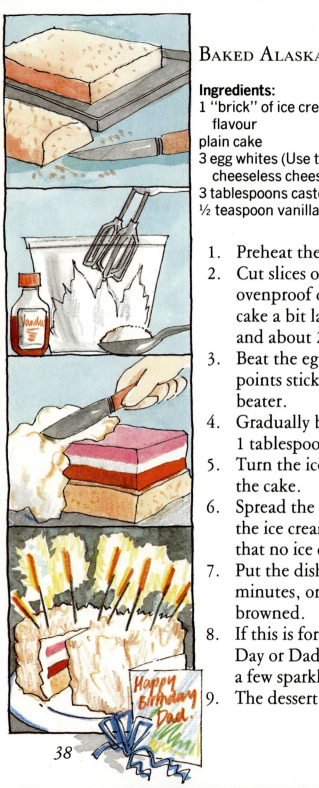

Baked Alaska

Ingredients:
1 "brick" of ice cream, any flavour
plain cake
3 egg whites (Use the yolks for cheeseless cheesecakes!)
3 tablespoons caster sugar
½ teaspoon vanilla

Things you need:
bowl
ovenproof serving dish
egg separator
egg beater

1. Preheat the oven to 230°C.
2. Cut slices of cake and arrange them in the ovenproof dish so that you have a slab of cake a bit larger than the ice cream "brick", and about 2 cm thick.
3. Beat the egg whites until they have stiff points sticking up when you lift up the beater.
4. Gradually beat in the vanilla and the sugar, 1 tablespoon at a time.
5. Turn the ice cream out of its container onto the cake.
6. Spread the egg white mixture thickly over the ice cream and the cake edges. Make sure that no ice cream is showing.
7. Put the dish in the oven for about 5 minutes, or until the outside is nicely browned.
8. If this is for a special occasion like Mother's Day or Dad's birthday, serve the Alaska with a few sparklers stuck into it.
9. The dessert is served at once, cut into slices.

Clown sundaes for any day

Ingredients:
ice cream, any flavour
ice cream cones
whipped cream
lollies for faces (hundreds and thousands, sliced jubes, Smarties, chocolate-covered sultanas, Lifesavers, or whatever else you like.)

Things you need:
ice cream scoop
plate

1. Put a dollop of stiffly whipped cream on a plate.
2. Put a round scoop of ice cream on top of the cream, leaving a ripple of cream around the ice cream . . . so now you have a head on a collar. You can decorate the collar with hundreds and thousands.
3. Make a face on the ice cream, using whatever lollies you have chosen.
4. The cone is the clown's hat, so put it on last, and your clown is ready.

Top-of-the-pyramid sweet treats

Chocolate roughs

Ingredients:
200 g cooking chocolate
½ cup desiccated coconut
250 g crushed roasted nuts —
  unsalted peanuts or hazelnuts

Things you need:
double boiler
teaspoon
tray lined with
  greaseproof paper
spoon

1. Put some water in the bottom of the double boiler, making sure the bottom of the top part doesn't touch the water.
2. Put the pan over a low heat.
3. Put the chocolate, broken up into bits, in the top part of the double boiler and set it in place on top of the bottom part. Stir the chocolate now and then as it slowly melts.
4. When the chocolate has melted, turn off the heat and take the top part of the double boiler off the bottom part.
5. Add the coconut and nuts to the chocolate and stir the mixture all together.
6. Put heaped teaspoonfuls of the choc-nut mixture onto the greaseproof paper and leave the little mounds to set.

Coconut Ice

Ingredients:
500 g icing sugar
1 egg white
3 tablespoons condensed milk
1 cup desiccated coconut
pink food colouring

Things you need:
sifter
egg separator
small bowl
larger bowl
baking dish (25 cm by 8 cm)
egg beater
knife, spoon

1. Grease the baking dish lightly.
2. Sift the icing sugar into a bowl and make a well in the centre.
3. Beat the egg white in the small bowl until it is frothy.
4. Pour the egg white and the condensed milk into the well you made in the sugar, and mix it all together.
5. Stir in the coconut, half a cup at a time. Use your hands now.
6. Divide the mixture into two, and press one half firmly and evenly into the tin.
7. Make the other half pink with the food colouring, then press it lightly on top of the white half.
8. Leave it until it is set, then cut it into small rectangles or squares.

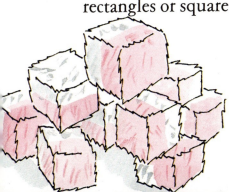

Apricot balls

Ingredients:
250 g dried apricots
½ can condensed milk
2 cups desiccated coconut
caster sugar

Things you need:
tin opener
scissors or knife
bowl
plate
spoon

1. Cut up the apricots into small pieces (scissors make cutting easier) and put them in a bowl.
2. Add the coconut to the bowl.
3. Add the condensed milk and mix everything together.
4. Roll the mixture into small balls, then roll the balls in a plate of caster sugar.

Gift-giving ideas

The sweet treats are great, easy-to-make gifts. Make just one kind, or give a combination of them. Here are some presentation ideas:

little basket

bowl

special mug

chocolate box, covered and re-used

cellophane bundle

mini garbage bin

Glossary of equipment

Glossary of ingredients

anchovies: very tiny fish with a strong flavour, tinned in oil
baking powder: a combination of several elements which make a dough puff up, or rise, when it is cooking
basil: *see herbs*
bicarbonate of soda: also known as "baking soda". It helps dough to rise, and is one of the elements in baking powder
blanched almonds: almonds which have had their skin removed after being soaked in boiling water. The skin of the almond is brown, while the blanched nut is white. Blanched means whitened
brown sugar: a light-brown powdery sugar
cabana: a spicy Italian sausage which can be eaten hot or cold
caster sugar: a sugar with very small light grains
cherry tomatoes: tiny tomatoes the size of cherries, generally sold in punnets like strawberries
chives: *see herbs*
coriander: *see herbs*
cumin: *see herbs*
desiccated coconut: the flesh of a coconut which has been grated and desiccated. Desiccated means dried
essence: very strong flavouring, so that you need very little
five-spice powder: a Chinese mixture of aniseed, fennel, pepper, cloves and cinnamon. It can be bought at the supermarket
gherkins: tiny cucumbers that have been pickled in sweet vinegar
glacé cherries: cherries that have been dipped in a sugar syrup
herbs: plants whose parts can be used to give extra flavour. Herbs can be fresh, dried or ground.

icing sugar: a white powder used for making icing
mixed herbs: a mixture of several dried herbs. *See herbs*
mixed peel: pieces of orange and lemon peel that have been dipped into a sugar syrup
mozzarella cheese: an Italian cheese that melts beautifully, forming stretchy bits when pulled apart
oregano: *see herbs*
parmesan cheese: a strong-smelling Italian cheese with a sharp taste. It is generally grated and sprinkled on spaghetti.
plain flour: white wheat flour that has no added baking powder
raw sugar: a light-brown, coarse-grained sugar
rice flour: a fine flour made from ground rice
rind: the coloured part of orange and lemon peel, sometimes called the "zest" because it is very strongly flavoured and a small amount adds a great deal of flavour to cooking
self-raising flour: white wheat flour that has baking powder mixed into it so that a dough or batter made with this will puff up, or "rise", when cooking
shallot: a type of onion, with a white root tip and a green stem and leaves
sour cream: this is not cream that is "off", but is purposely soured for the taste!
soy (or soya) sauce: a black sauce used a great deal in all Asian cooking, made from soya beans. The light soy is called "superior soy", and can be bought at supermarkets. The heavy soy is made with mushrooms as well as soya beans, and is called "mushroom soy". It is darker and has a stronger taste.
sugar: a sweetener made from sugarcane
thyme: *see herbs*

Glossary of cooking words

boil: to heat liquid until it bubbles very busily

chop: to cut things up quite small, generally into cube-like pieces

floury surface: a pastry board or clean table top, lightly sprinkled and rubbed over with flour to prevent dough sticking to it

fry: to heat small amount of oil or butter in a pan and cook food in the hot oil or butter

grease: to rub butter or margarine lightly all over the inside of a dish or tin using a crumpled paper towel or something similar. This prevents whatever you're cooking from sticking

preheat: to turn on an oven some time before you put the food in so that there is time for the oven to reach the temperature needed

rub in: one way to mix butter and flour together when making a dough: to rub the butter chunks and the flour together over and over between your fingers and thumbs until everything is mixed together and looks like breadcrumbs

simmer: to turn the heat down low after the liquid has begun to boil so that the bubbles are kept small and gentle

slice: to cut things into long thin pieces. These pieces are called slices

turn out a cake: to remove the cake from the cake tin by turning the rack upside down on top of the cake tin and turning the tin upside down. To do this, you should use oven mitts. Make sure you hold the rack firmly against the tin. The cake should slide out of the tin, so that you can lift the tin off, leaving the cake on the rack